The Garden He Planted

Melanie Ware

For my Pops

TABLE OF CONTENTS

My Father's Daughter

Questions	1
Faith	3
Beginnings	6
Dirt	10
Kings Canyon	11
Dodgeball	13
An Upside Down Christmas Tree	16
Hospitals	18
Shattered	20
Midnight Phone Call	23
Turtle Tears	25
Early Morning Drives	35
Mouse Therapy	37
The Break of a Wave	39
ABC	43
Lecture Hall Flirting	47
Stars	49
Bench Talk	52
Abstinence	55
Sunrise	57

Under the Eucalyptus Trees   61
Acknowledgements   69

"The difference between the man who just cuts lawns and a real gardener is in the touching. The lawn cutter might just as well not have been there at all; the gardener will be there a lifetime."

- Ray Bradbury, *Fahrenheit 451*

MY FATHER'S DAUGHTER

I

QUESTIONS

"Why?" James whispered soft but determined and like always, I couldn't find the words to respond.

Birds had started to sing through the rectangular windows, their tone somewhere between doleful and delighted. Dawn, with it's misty grey shadows and cool stagnant air, trickled in above us as we spoke in quiet voices that always seem appropriate when the only sounds around are shy chirps. The rest of his housemates wouldn't be awake for another few hours, so we enjoyed the briskness of spring in Santa Cruz.

"Mel, there has to be a reason you believe that," he let out with a tired sigh as an exhausted smile played on his lips. His black hair stood at odd angles and his soft brown cheeks still had marks from the creases in his pillowcase. Our conversations usually ran around in circles; his determination kept him going, my stubbornness kept me quiet. *Why do I believe there is a God? Why do I believe that the Bible's word is true? Why, why, why?* All these answers I thought I knew failed me now. *What else would I lose if I lost this faith? Would*

1

all those things that made me a Christian cease to be important?

I don't know. That was really all I could think to say. The last year and a half, freshman year of college and now a few months into sophomore year, had been full of "I don't know"s. *I don't know what I believe anymore. Did I ever really? I don't know if we should date. But we're going to. I don't know if I know who I am anymore. My existential crisis.* I was a struggling Christian holding onto a faith I feared I was losing. I couldn't say it to him, because I couldn't even say it to myself.

James knew my past. He had met my family, heard my stories, seen old photos. But something was missing for him. To everything I said, he had something to say back. He kept it going. He always wanted to know more.

I flipped over to look at him, tears creating a watery vision of his bewildered face.

FAITH

My dad was a spiritual man. He'd gone through a Nietzsche stage and I'm sure a few others, but that all happened before I was born. It wasn't until we lived momentarily in Venice Beach that I really realized what it meant to live a Christian life. He didn't look nor act like those clean-cut business men Christians who give money to charity and go to church every Sunday because it's what they're suppose to do. He was a dirty hippie surfer and enjoyed having long talks with the Venice beach homeless. His beard and mustache grew wild and his eyebrow piercing and tattoo maybe made him intimidating at first. People probably mistook him for a homeless man a few times.

We lived in Venice with my dad two times during my childhood. The first was in an empty apartment that belonged a man named Sherman that my dad worked with. Right when you walked in a huge staircase welcomed you. We'd get in our sleeping bags and ride down them like tobogganing on a snowy hill. The second round seemed like some crazy miracle to a twelve year

3

old me. It was the summer before I started junior high and Lilly entered high school. A man my dad somehow knew needed to leave the country to film a show and he asked my dad to housesit his fully furnished apartment. I don't remember how long we stayed there but the people of Venice took to my dad's charm so we were always welcomed back. In fact, a mural dedicated to him covers a wall in the backyard of his quirky friend's house. Lucky for us, the apartment was right on the edge of Venice beach; we could see the waves from the living room. Lilly and I spent all day getting sunburned and scootering around the boardwalk in our bathing suits. We had our usual pizza place with the blue walls and broken down chairs that knew what we wanted the second we walked in. My dad trusted us enough to let us roam freely. We sat in the sand and ate ice cream as the tourists with their cameras and henna tattoos walked by.

Meanwhile, my dad was busy listening to the life story of some man who most people didn't see, or chose not to see. He would sit with these men and women for hours, sharing Bible verses and showing his dedication to God. I picture him kneeling in front of a man with wild hair and skin leathered from the constant Southern California sun. The man was probably relating his life in a stream of consciousness. Few people would take this time, so I imagined he wanted to get everything out. Everything he'd been thinking about since he ended up on the gum-covered streets of Venice. Regrets maybe, past loves, a family he lost. And my dad would listen intently, holding on to each word said, comforting him through Bible verses and his own stories. He read a more modern version of the Bible called *The Message* and always carried it with him. Inside were notes scribbled along the margins and underlines and highlights. It probably lie open on the grassy ground as he flipped through it trying to find the right passage for that particular moment. Maybe he read out encouraging words, like "Wait on the Lord; be of good courage, and He shall strengthen your heart" (Psalm 27: 13-14).

BEGINNINGS

Rhonda Davis and Doug Ware met when she was 22 and he was 26. My dad had dared his brother Bob to talk to that cute blonde, tan girl working at the hair salon. When he chickened out, my dad, with surfer boy charm and thick hair, did it. She said yes. Nine months later, they were married. Five years later my sister was born and a year and a half later I came along.

I remember family trips to Mammoth in the summer, laying in the attic and watching our lizards eat flies from the windows. I learned how to ride a bike on the uneven path on the way to the cabin and Lilly and I sat under the bridge burping our ABCs. Or our annual trips to Lake Nacimiento, making fishing poles out of sticks and swimming in murky water. I remember going to my Nana's condo in Laguna Beach and falling asleep to the ocean. I remember living in the garage of my dad's clients home after our property in the Malibu hills burned down. That house tucked away in Lobo Canyon and how when it rained the driveway flooded. He renovated the garage so that there were three rooms; a bathroom, kitchen/parents bedroom/living room and then a room for Lilly and I. I remember swimming in that pool at night, catching snakes in the yard and the swing that went over the mountain side. I remember moving to Thousand Oaks. I remember my parents yelling in the kitchen while I threw basketballs in a hoop outside. I remember slammed doors and pretending I hadn't heard anything.

When I was eight, they separated.

My dad had a thing for garages. As an artist and a contractor I think he preferred living in something he could easily mold into his own haven. A run-down unused space that he could turn into a vibrant unusual home. An unconventional place for an unconventional man. So instead of moving out right away, my dad took to spending time in the garage that also acted as his studio. Sometimes, late at night, I'd sneak into it when I knew my mom lay asleep in the house. To get inside I had to open the two wall-sized light blue front doors and skillfully close them at the same time to keep them shut. By the light of the moon I could see paint and canvases littered on the ground. The glowing red light from the darkroom was off.

I don't know if he expected me, little eight-year-old me with my thin framed glasses and frizzy hair slyly pulling apart these huge doors. I would tiptoe in and lay down on the futon beside him and feel safe, like there was no better place in the world to be than right here. We shared the same thick brown hair, the same smile that never looked forced, even if it was.

My relationship with my mom and Lilly was different. Where I felt included and understood with him, I felt neglected and left-out with them. One morning before school, when the sky glowed grey with clouds and I was finishing up eating breakfast, the two of them rushed towards me and tried to push me out the back sliding glass door. I struggled and they succeeded, forcing me into the cold morning air. As I pounded my hands against the door, I could clearly see their laughing faces, both with blonde hair, and same oval face. I started to cry. My sister was my mother's daughter. I was my father's daughter. At least this is how I saw it.

Finally, when I was nine, they got a divorce. They had pulled me and Lilly away from the TV to tell us and sat so their heads were level with ours. They spoke in clear, gentle words. "It's not your fault," they said. The classic divorce statement. It didn't really phase me like it did my sister and I asked if I could go back to the living room. Perhaps my thoughts were selfish, but I saw their divorce as a positive event, one in which allowed me to spend time with just my dad. He moved into the garage in Burbank, my mom stayed in Thousand Oaks. He got us on the weekends and Wednesdays, she got us during the rest of the week.

DIRT

With my dad, we were outdoor kids. We ran dirty fingered and dirty skinned through camp grounds and forests, with long sticks and baggy overalls. We crawled through caves in Red Rock with pocket knives, searching for animals bones. We slept dry under a lean-to in the Sequoias as the rain fell on and rolled off the bright blue tarp. We cuddled together and watched movies in my dad's Snug Top when we got too cold. We went to sleep under a clear Wyoming sky and woke to a foot of snow. We ate "the regular;" ground beef, Deluxe Mac and Cheese and baked beans. We lay beneath eucalyptus trees on a deserted island and made friends with strangers. We knew how good we had it.

KINGS CANYON

I sat in the passenger seat of my mom's white Jeep with my arms crossed and bitterness in my eyes. I stared out the window, my breath fogging up the glass and watched the rain splash the road. I don't remember many days with only my mom during my childhood. Maybe my mind was so focused on the desire of having adventures with my dad. The two of us had gone out to lunch. My dad had taken Lilly on a backpacking trip in Kings Canyon and the jealousy ate at me. I was too young, he told me. I wouldn't be able to carry enough on my back but when I was older, he promised we would have our own trip. We never did though.

I feel like my mom sat there looking at me, trying to think of something to say or do that would make us bond. She said that she'd heard of a singer, Christina Aguilera, and that we should go get her CD and listen to it on the drive home. She pulled into a mall and we went to the entertainment store. I walked through the aisles, imagining the two of them out there in the wilderness, thinking about all the fun they were having and I wasn't.

She found it and back in the car we listened. I see now that she tried but I was just too stubborn. I would tell myself that this would to turn out boring, I would resent this weekend and that my mom was no fun. I wanted to be in Burbank or camping, but instead I sat with folded arms looking out a rainy window.

DODGEBALL

We came to realize that Burbank in the summer brings only heat. Lilly, then thirteen or fourteen and I, probably twelve, turned the sprinkler on under the trampoline and began playing a makeshift dodgeball game. We giggled and fell and slipped. Lilly's blond hair was quickly turning brown the wetter it got, and my face was getting redder the hotter it got. The garage window, the one located right above my dad's bed, spread open wide to the backyard. Music whirled through and mingled with our laughter.

We faintly heard our names called. We curled our feet when we jumped off the trampoline because spiky little weeds covered the ground and the brick walkway burned with the midday sun. Still dripping, we hobbled inside the open door.

The dry-wall to the left of the door was covered in notes, numbers and doodles my dad scribbled in colorful pens while on the phone, when we still had landlines. Instead of carpet or hardwood beneath our feet a huge beige rug lay, woven out of some natural material that made the garage smell faintly of hay. His colorful paintings lined the walls, walls that after years never got painted and never would. Where the wall and ground met were homemade cabinets that held books on Van Gogh and Picasso. Our hammocks from Mexico hung from the lofts my dad made for me and Lilly. The garage was just one huge room, so he built the lofts to give us privacy but we rarely felt like climbing their ladders and suffocating from the rising heat. Instead we just had our mattresses, with their checkered comforters, on the floor.

We moved past the little red couch at the foot of my dad's bed, the one I so often found myself reading and sleeping on, and plopped down with our backs against the wall, facing him. He sat down quietly in front of us. Looking back there was a tension in the air, but at the time I paid little attention to it.

"Ok, some good news, and some bad news" he said. His messy pony tail at the nape of his neck had little strands of hair escaping. "We're going to Hawaii!" Another trip to add to our large list of adventures. Lilly and I giggled in excitement and then turned back to him for the bad news. It couldn't be *that* bad.

"Bad news is, girls, I have skin cancer."

I vaguely remember the details of the rest of

the afternoon. Lilly asked him questions and he answered them the best he could. He said something about not knowing how bad it was or how much time he had left.

Something in me knew at that moment that he would die. My best friend, my role model, my Pops. Time paused; looking at him I saw all the things I knew I would miss play in front of me, all the things he would miss. Going to Alaska, home schooling out of a trailer as we made our way across the U.S. Visions of what the future skipped through my mind and disappeared out of sight for fear of their reality. All the backpacking and camping trips that we had yet to go on. He wouldn't be there when I fell in love for the first time, or to talk to about religion and fight with about whatever fathers and daughters fight about. Looking at him in that moment, with his eyebrow piercing and long nose, I saw a life lost and a time, a huge chapter in my life, soon gone.

CHRISTMAS

One year, sometime before we found out about the cancer, we hung the Christmas tree upside down from the ceiling in the space between the two lofts. How my dad did it, I can't remember. The whole space filled with the scent of pine as we set up our beds and most likely watched a movie. Lilly and I slept in the middle of the floor, directly under the lit and ornamented tree, somehow not afraid it would fall on us in the night. It could have been trust, but maybe just exhaustion.

When we woke up, a wall of presents surrounded us. I remember looking around and not being able to see the floor, only the walls with all the paintings. Our faces lit up, not at the excitement of presents, but of the shock and awe of waking up to a wrapping paper castle. We began at the top, opening and laughing as we went.

Most of them were just empty boxes covered in shinny red and gold paper. Some large ones had just a piece of candy while others had little things from the 99 Cent Store, like pencils, notepads and stickers. A few Mexican trinkets, miniature dolls or hair clips, hid in crumpled up tissue paper, waiting to be found.

The rest of that day the floor stayed littered with red and gold wrapping paper.

HOSPITALS

For a while, time proceeded just as before. We stayed with him on the weekends and he came to Thousand Oaks on Wednesdays. But there was a sense of urgency now that we all felt. Then the cancer was spreading fast and he had a 3% survival rate. He developed a tumor on his shoulder and called it mini-me. He joked about his problems, because that was all he could do. "It's all good," he would say over and over. What happens will come. What the future held, no one knew.

After the Hawaii trip we stopped going places. Our days of camping in Wyoming and the Redwoods ended. Living at Malibu Creek State Park on the weekends stopped. All those sketchy and exhilarating trips to Mexico were just memories now. After a while, he no longer came on Wednesdays. Shortly after that he was admitted to a hospital, which meant no more weekends in Burbank.

I saw a picture of him in the MRI, the tests with the tubes going into his lungs and the CAT scan visits. A tumor in his lung, tumors on his skull, little lumps that made it hard to wash his hair. Appointment after appointment, in and out of the hospital every week. The details of these hospital trips are all muddled now. Except for when I walked into his room and Braveheart was playing on the TV. Mel Gibson cheers on the Scots, saying the other side could take his life, but not his freedom. My dad laughed in his bed and said something I can't remember that made us all laugh too.

SHATTERED

The hospice building was small with an amalgamation of flowers under every window and a small parking lot. The walls inside and out glowed a yellowish green and light wafted in from open windows. It appeared a pleasant place, relaxing and comforting. The nurses all smiled as I walked by, my big bulky headphones on my head; the wires getting lost in my long smooth brown hair. I was a tomboy by all means, except when it came to my hair. I wore Dickies or jeans and band shirts everyday. I owned no shorts or skirts or dresses. I never wore makeup or jewelry. With my hairstylist mom, I got it permanently straightened and made sure every morning it fell perfectly in place.

I held my testy walkman steadily in my hands so it wouldn't skip. Pete Yorn's firm yet soft somber voice filtered through my ears, singing "I'm gonna lose you." I listened intently. Even though his songs were slightly melancholic and maybe too mature for a thirteen year old girl they comforted me. Sometimes sad songs are just the right things to listen to to make me content. Ever since he started going to hospitals I'd started to listen to this CD. It was my mom's and I'm sure none of my classmates even knew he existed. I knew even then that it would be the soundtrack to this point in my life.

On my way to his room, the walkman slipped out of my hands. In slow motion, the CD spat out and shattered as it hit the checkered lanolin floor. Ok, so maybe CDs don't shatter, but in my memory it did. Maybe the walkman shattered, I guess that would make more sense. I stood there and I stared at it. The nurses came around to help me pick it up and I just ran. Where I ran to I don't remember, probably the bathroom. The CD breaking showed my life falling apart one track at a time. I composed myself and let that little shock wear off and returned to my dad's room. He lay there laughing with my sister. His face no longer glowed the way it used to. But his fire wasn't fading out and I doubt it ever did. On his bedside table sat *The Message*, more torn up and worn out than I'd ever seen it. He anticipated death, I think his faith was so strong that he had always been ready to go. Seeing him like that, so positive at such a serious event, made me realize it would be alright. How could I lament his death when I knew he was ready to go, when I knew he was at peace with his death?

From that night on, my faith changed. Every night before I fell asleep, I'd close my eyes and hold my hands and pray the exact same prayer: "Dear Lord, I know that he is going to die, and I'm ok with that. But please let me and Lilly come out alright. Let us become stronger because of it. Amen." And I'd drift off into a dream with a faint smile on my face.

MIDNIGHT PHONE CALL

A little over a year after he'd told us about he cancer, the phone rang. I had spent a week of sleepless nights waiting for this sound. My hair lay sprawled on my pillow, a brown mess from tossing about. The sound didn't come as a surprise, but still my heart's calm quickly turned to chaos. *Brrrinnggg.* I rolled over. The air felt hot, the onset of Spring in Southern California had begun. Outside my shuttered window, the moon illuminated the fence and came close to drowning out the stars. I wondered how those stars must feel; so infinite just slung in this seemingly dark world of the great universal abyss. I knew I could never understand their existence and their vastness. I knew there were a lot of things I couldn't comprehend. Like what happens when a star dies?

It rang again. Through the crack under our door I could see the living room light switch on. The sound of my mom's hurried footsteps along the wood floor echoed; I listened hard, without needing too. I knew what the phone call meant.

"Is it...?" Silence. Her voice shook: "Ok, thanks

for calling... Thank you. I'm gonna tell the girls." I heard the faint click of the phone returning to the dock and my mom sit down on the coffee table.

I assumed Lilly was already awake in the bed beside me. We shared a tiny room that was just big enough for our beds to fit in. Sleepless nights most likely plagued her as well. We lay there silently, straining our ears as my mom took a rest before coming into our room. I imagined her: elbows on her knees, face in her hands. What was she thinking? Were memories of her own flooding into her head? The door creaked open as she softly entered. A dim light expanded across the yellow wall in front of me. I stayed still.

"Girls?" A pause. She knew we were awake. How unfortunate it is to be the bearer of bad news. I silently struggled. My heart slowed again, but I couldn't suppress the approaching emptiness. How do you tell your children their father just died? In some far off place, far away from where I was then, she muttered: "Girls, he's gone."

TURTLE TEARS

Once, in Mexico, my bearded dragon Lizzy ran away. We had left him and Rocko, Lilly's lizard, out on the beach in these woven baskets in the shade. In retrospect, not a great idea. We left for a moment and when we came back, there was a hole right through the side and he was nowhere to be found. The day we had moved into our house in Thousand Oaks, our mom and dad had presented us with tiny baby lizards and somehow, within minutes, I lost mine. He wasn't even Lizzy yet. Months, or was it weeks, later, when my dad was getting a broom from the backyard, there was Lizzy, twice the size we had last seen him.

Another time, we lay on the beach at night and when we dipped our feet in the water, crabs bit at our toes. We said goodbye to day with an orange sunset and fell asleep to the sound of waves. We drove around on top of my dad's truck, holding onto the space between the Snug Top and the cab. We made trips to an orphanage, bringing massive amounts of toilet paper, canned food and stuffed animals. I remember giving one of my Beanie

Babies to a little girl who smiled and thanked me with such enthusiasm I thought she might squeal.

But this time, when I was ten, we went for three weeks instead of the usual three or four days. We even flew there and rented an old VW Bug. The blue paint was chipping, the cushions in the seats were popping out and it felt dirty. We drove all night until we came to this secluded beach that had a huge cement building and a hut or two on the sand. This was our "hotel." No one spoke English, so my dad had to make due with broken Spanish, smiles and enthusiastic hand gestures. The stairs were on the outside of the cement slab and our room was on the top floor. Well, more like it was the top floor. Inside were two beds, mismatched sheets and pillows, a balcony that overlooked the ocean and a bathroom.

Every morning we drove to this little convenience store meets cafe. It was the only place in miles that had air conditioning and in that heat we were desperate. Lilly and I would get juice and even though I was allergic, I always got watermelon. We walked around the tiny store like we owned it, sipping our drinks and flipping through postcards. We watched tourists filter in and out and we tried to make friends with the cashier. We left one day with my dad telling us he had met someone who was going to show us a very special treat.

He had a knack for that, for meeting people and working his way into amazing experiences that would never have happened otherwise. I think his constant positive attitude gave off some energy that people were drawn to. Lilly would inherent this trait. While she would envy my ability to make friends fast, I would be envious of how she always managed to weasel her way into trips and jobs.

This particular man, whose name I wish I could remember, was Mexican but spoke perfect English. Much further down the beach from our cement home, a massive resort hotel, with bright lights, loud parties and air conditioning, glittered against the waves. As the resident doctor for the place, he knew all sort of exciting things that were going on.

One night when it was near a full moon, we drove with him to a remote beach. We walked quietly down the sand with two other men while he pointed out to us what the netted off sections meant. They were where mother sea turtles had already come up to lay their eggs. These areas were heavily guarded by conservation efforts to protect the nests from snatchers, people who would take the eggs and sell them, as well as animals who ate them. We continued to walk and in the glimmer of moonlight, we saw, moving her way slowly up the sand, a huge female sea turtle. Approaching with as little noise as possible, we sat and watched as she began to dig out the sand and lay her perfect, glistening white, tender eggs into a pile in the hole. He told us that when a sea turtle lays her eggs, she sheds a tear for them. We looked at her eyes and they were wet, the sand clumping around the edges. She had to let go of her babies, never to see them again and hoping against all odds they would make it. She couldn't keep them safe anymore or teach them all she knew about the wild. The men then helped her into the ocean and we went back to our beds to dream about the turtles hatching.

That dream turned reality about a week later. The man came by to tell us that one of the nests had hatched. As a part of the resorts special perks, when the first nest hatched they had a ceremony. We wandered down the beach and on the sand were paper bags with candles in them that lined a path down to the ocean. The lights were dull so that the moon and its reflection was a stronger guide to the water for the little guys.

All the kids got small paper bags. When I was handed mine, I could hear miniature flippers scratching at the edges, brand new eyes trying to figure out which way to go. I peeked into it and saw the tiniest turtle, the size of my palm, moving around. No one was allowed to touch them, which is torture when you hold in your hand the most perfect creature you've ever seen. A feeling of excitement that makes you smile to the point where it hurts. When we were given the word to let them go, we gently put the bags to the ground and tipped them over. The beach was covered in hushed excitement, eyes lit up with anticipation, until we saw those uncoordinated bodies emerge. We had to be entirely careful to watch our little guys, make sure they got to the water but still not touching them. They zig zagged, tripped over their own miniature arms and took breaks, tired from this new adventure. We stood at the edge of the calm water and in the reflection of the moon could see little black dots in the bubbling, gentle white water. And when they disappeared, we all wished them good luck because we knew they needed it. They were being thrown into a new world with no one to guide them but instincts.

EARLY MORNING DRIVES

The summer before my Freshman year of high school we moved to live with my aunt in Simi Valley. Lilly had a job back in Thousand Oaks and my best friend Chris lived there who I would rather spend my days with than in the hot, empty Simi Valley. I'd get in the car probably around eight in the morning; the air was already becoming humid and hot and the sky always seemed to be red. For some reason, there were only three CDs in her car: All-American Rejects, Death Cab For Cutie, and last but not least was a CD by The Cure. By some miracle, listening to these same songs all summer brought Lilly and I together. Maybe it had nothing to do with the music, maybe it was just because this was the most time we had spent together. Just the two of us and no one else. I had gone on for so long believing that we were two completely different people with little in common. But she went through what I went through. We had shared a childhood, a father, a death. We had dived into crystal clear cenotes and climbed the stairs of Mayan ruins in the Yucatán Peninsula.

We were always referred to as "the girls." "Oh, how are the girls doing?" or "What are the girls up to." "He was a father who left a legacy to his girls." We were one word, not Lillian and Melanie, but Girls. Our conjoined name, so often considered one even though that was the last thing we wanted. I had always pushed that aside, constantly trying to be my own person. And while I still felt that way and we were both entirely different people, we still joined together as sisters. It only took our father's death and a few car rides to notice the importance of that.

MOUSE THERAPY

It started with bitter car rides. I wouldn't talk to my mom about my thoughts and feelings on his death. I did not keep it all bottled up. I had close friends who had looked up to him as a father figure that listened to me and felt my loss. But I think she thought it her motherly responsibility to send me to therapy.

The waiting room had dark brown wood and in his office was a massive window that looked out on the busy streets below. I sat on the couch and held a pillow out of discomfort and awkwardness. These sessions were unbearable and cliché. He looked like a mouse with glasses and when he wrote notes on his clip board I wanted to get up and slam it out of his hands. He asked me and-how-does-that-make-you-feel? kind of questions and more than anything I wanted to tell him to fuck off.

My mom would be there in the waiting room when I got out. At first, I couldn't even bear to look at her out of anger and annoyance. It seemed unnecessary and obnoxious. Once again I'd cross my arms and look out the window, but it wasn't raining and instead the sun hit the pavement outside. Then I started talking to her about his stupid mouse face and his full of shit ways. She'd laugh and genuinely care and after just a few trips there she decided I didn't need him after all. She saw I was doing alright and something in her had changed.

On the way to school every morning freshman year, we talked and listened to our favorite radio duo, Kevin and Bean. When she picked me up, I told her about how awful running the mile was because my face stayed red all day or how Honors Geometry was killing me slowly.

It didn't all happen in a day but over the span of a year or two, she seemed let go. Maybe she was coming to terms with both her daughters being in high school and growing up, or it could be that she recognized I never quite felt comfortable around her. Maybe after her own father died, my grandpa who used to help us climb trees and play tag, she understood how it felt. Maybe she saw how crazy her friends' children were and she was just thankful her girls didn't fall into that category. Whatever it was, she began to relax.

THE BREAK OF A WAVE

My sophomore, junior and senior years of high school all seemed to blend together in a mix and steady flow of church, surf and swim. After switching high schools two days before tenth grade, I finally felt I had found my niche. I discovered myself and friends in the youth group I went to with Lilly every Wednesday and Sunday. We had a large group of friends, mixed with all grades and year by year we lost more and more to graduations so that by my senior year the group was down to about six of us.

We all remember "that one Tuesday morning" because something about it was so profound and inspiring and unique that nothing ever came close to it. I remember my alarm going off at around six in the morning, grabbing my surf bag and my long board with the twin blue stripes. This was my escape from school, from stress, from responsibility. We went before school and after, on weekends and at night when the phosphorescence was so bright we looked like shooting stars on the waves.

We parked and jumped out of the car and

walked down to the shore. Silhouettes against a painted sky. Behind the pier that seemed to stretch endlessly, was an explosion of colors. In this moment, the whole world seemed to stop. Never had I seen such brilliant colors in front of me; blue mingled with the intense strokes of vermillion and orange with lighting yellow and a color that seemed to be all those wrapped in one. I felt truly connected with God.

Back at the car, we unloaded the boards and pulled our wetsuits on. I strapped my leash to my left ankle, and headed down the rocks. The water flowed over us, cold but invigorating feeling something like music; the rhythm of the water, swaying from the shore, back to us.

Now no worldly things plagued my mind. We were all a part of nature, one with the ocean and with each other. At times like these I felt stronger than ever in my faith because I could feel the presence of God. I usually took time to thank Him when I got out into the water on any given day, but today was a different kind of thankfulness. Everything felt perfect. I couldn't think of one aspect about this morning that I would have changed and It was moments like these that I felt secure with my faith and that this is where I was meant to be in life. Because I was intwined with nature, with the vast ocean and holy sky, I felt intwined with my religion. These moments out in the water I sensed my dad. Maybe it was just that I assumed if he were still alive, he would be out there with us, telling us stories about surf trips he took to Mexico and Africa and telling me how happy he was that I loved surfing as much as he did. My best friend Jenayl always said that she knew my dad because she could see him in me. It was the combination of experiencing two of his favorite things, God and surfing, that made me feel so strong and at peace. Everything just felt right.

And something about the act of surfing liberated me from the world. The second I would feel the wave grab hold of my board I knew what was coming. At moments like this, my mind goes slightly blank and instinct takes over. *Paddle, paddle paddle, push, stand up.* I imagined God's huge hand pushing my board like a dad does for his child. Encouraging them, "Yea, you've got this! Just keep paddling!" Then would come the drop-in where I took control and painted bubbles in the face of the wave with my tail fins. Such a feeling I have yet to experience with anything else. A mix between complete freedom, total focus and the release of letting everything go.

The sun still hadn't risen all the way and the

brilliant fusion of colors still spread above us. We reluctantly headed into shore and for one last moment, we all stood there and looked out at the picturesque seaside. We merged onto the freeway, all our voices mingled together as each of us told details of our best wave or some injury or how our fingers were finally thawing. Our laughter poured out of the rolled down windows as we relived the hours that had just passed.

ABC

After a blissful summer of working for a surf camp and spending more time at the beach than my own house, it was time for me to take the five hour drive from southern to northern California and begin my life as a college student. University of California, Santa Cruz was where I always knew I wanted to go and so the second my feet touched the cement of my residential college Stevenson, I felt perfectly at home. I looked around me and saw towering redwoods, excited faces, surfboards and deer. *Man, I kept thinking, my dad would love it here.* In the following week I would sleep in the woods, participate in endless dance parties disguised as protests, sleep as little as possible and meet more entertaining people than I ever had before. Santa Cruz, in my eyes, was perfect.

Of course I had been warned about the liberal nature of the town and university, but I was dedicated to my religion and I felt confident I would be fine. And I kept telling myself this over and over as the weeks went on and I started doubting whether I really would be fine.

Sometime in those first few weeks I met my neighbor in the dorms Greg. He had awkward curly hair, loved John Frusciante and once referred to himself as an Italian Stallion. Or maybe we called him that and he hated it. We would communicate between our rooms by playing Earth, Wind, and Fire or Jackson 5 through the windows or by knocking on the wall; one for yes, two for no, three for come over, etc. Sometimes my roommate would leave for the weekend and we would have sleepovers. Not like the "grown-up" definition, but the play-date ten-year-old version.

"So, do you know a guy named James Sutter?" I asked him during our first sleep-over. Classes had already started and we were settling into our new college life. It seemed like each day I met at least five new people from Stevenson and so I figured Greg had to and might know my new crush.

"Hmm what does he look like?"

"Black hair, Ray-Bans, peacoat..."

"Maybe... why?"

"Well... He's in my Core class and he may be the most attractive guy I've seen here," I admitted like a little gossiping fifth-grader. All freshman UCSC students had to take a core class through their college. Stevenson was the only one required two quarters, and our topic was "Self and

Society." Our readings were extensive and thought-provoking, ranging from the Bible to Jean-Paul Sartre and existentialism, to Marx and the Tao.

"Is he nice and respectful?" he asked like a concerned parent.

I admitted I didn't know him well but he seemed intelligent and courteous.

We talked about relationships and people we've dated. We occasionally glanced at the clock on the microwave and were always surprised at how much time had passed. The conversation moved onto our families and he asked me about mine. I gave him the run-down: Mom, dad, sister. Divorce.. and then I paused.

"Well, actually my dad is dead" I said. He was the first person at Santa Cruz I'd shared this with.

"Wait... really?" he said softly. I couldn't see his expression because it was somewhere around four or five in the morning and no light shone through the widows. Usually people tell me they're sorry for my loss. Or that it must be hard and that we don't have to talk about it. I hate that and I felt relieved when he didn't. His tone sounded odd, not really surprised, though there was some of that in there too.

"Yea, when I was thirteen. From skin cancer."

"Ummm... this is really weird." I didn't know what he was talking about started to get nervous and self-conscious.

"Why?"

"Because my mom died when I was thirteen too."

At seven in the morning we finally fell asleep. I had shared with him all my growing religious concerns. I had always disagreed with a few aspects of the Bible, like condemning homosexuals and strictly obeying your parents. But what if they were abusive or unfit as a parent? How is it possible that a community so open that claims to love all people can not accept the gay community? And I told him that I had begun poking holes in my own religion. Core was making me realize that I had never given other philosophical or religious beliefs much thought, so how could I know Christianity was for me? He said he thought it was healthy that I didn't whole-heartedly believe everything in the Bible and that to really believe in something you have to question it. Right then I knew my dad would have loved him. My dad had never pressured Lilly and I to be Christians. He showed by example and because of this I believe he would have been happy to see me struggling.

LECTURE HALL FLIRTING

I spent late nights in the library, the one by the dorms that, until about a week before, would stay open 24/7. We were a wild group of freshmen and took advantage of the hours to throw a full out party inside once the campus security officers had left for the night. It resulted in speakers being confiscated, drunk kids being written up and the building closing at 2:00 am.

James and I collected our belongings when the custodian came in to kick us out. I remembered something an older student told me, that sometimes they forget to lock the lecture rooms. So we ventured into the brisk outdoors and tried the first one we came across. In the darkness, we twisted the cold handle, and slowly pushed it open. We looked around, whispered and lay on the floor with only the light from our computers. We watched The Daily Show and talked about art. I was fascinated by him because I couldn't compare him to anyone I met or fit him into a category of people. He spoke his mind freely and honestly and was both confident and unsure of himself. We were nervous and shy and as the light outside changed from black to grey, we stood up and folded blankets. He played music on his phone, I cat walked across a table in front of the blackboard and we went to the dining hall where we waited until they opened, then curled up on the comfy chairs and watched a movie.

A few days later we would kiss at 7:00 am after falling asleep during a movie in highly uncomfortable positions. He'd pass me a note card that said "Would you like to go out and see a movie?" We'd see Fantastic Mr. Fox and hold hands on the bus. We would sit next to each other in class and have breakfast in the dining hall at 8:00 am every morning. We'd flirt, I'd get drunk for the first time after my last final and then we'd break up the day before winter break.

STARS

I grabbed my jacket and put sweats on over my pants then shuffled through the random things under my dorm room bed until I found my sleeping bag. My steps were quick and my head down, determination and hysterics preventing me from talking to anyone I passed. The leaves on the ground fluttered under my feet and my hair whisked around my face. I reached the knoll that over looks the Monterey Bay and threw my sleeping bag down in the tall grasses so I lay hidden. I burrowed into it and pulled out my journal and began writing fast and scribbled thoughts.

I questioned why some days I felt so ecstatic about life and my place in it. But then others I wanted to be alone and away from people. *Maybe this is all part of growing up,* I wrote. My views kept changing and my indecisive nature seemed to be a problem. An odd sort of rage ran through me and through my pen. *Am I just angry at myself for bursting like this? Is it my fault for keeping all this inside?* I felt like I was losing this "innocence" that I had always been trying to hold onto. By not drinking or smoking or having sex I believed that I still had some kind of innocence. I knew that was a lie I told myself, like I actually wanted to be ignorant.

The fierce wind shook the trees as they moaned faintly. I felt like them. All those things I had been so comfortable believing and staying true to were being shaken and questioned from inside and out. For the last few years I had been so attached to my little Christian bubble that I forgot much of the world didn't share my views. Maybe I just didn't want to think about a world outside of what I knew. *Does being a Christian define me? Would I still be me without it? Is it ok to be wrong when you are talking to yourself?*

I rolled over onto my back and stared up at the full moon and the almost clear sky. The chill of the air stung my face and the tall grasses that surrounded me did little to block the wind. I studied the stars, wanting to escape my thoughts. Years ago, my dad would take us to the desert and we'd lay with our head on his outstretched arms. We'd look up at the stars and I remember thinking that I never want to do this with any other man again. A part of me hoped I would see a vision of my dad in the constellations giving me advice. I think he would have told me that I had to go through this and that it was part of the perpetual questioning of life. But I wanted to know if it ever got easier.

I thought about the other people looking at the stars that night. Out of the seven billion people on this planet, there must have been thousands doing the same thing. The tiny sparkle of lights below in the city and the reflection of the moon on the ocean generously shed light on the scene around me. Were people in those houses eating dinner? Watching a movie? Having sex? Scribbling away in journals? *I'm not the only person thinking this right now. I'm not alone.* But maybe this wasn't that comforting to me. Secretly, maybe I wanted to be alone. To prove to myself and others that I was strong enough to discover what religion meant to me now. *I am strong.* That prayer I said every night during my dad's sickness came back to me: "Please let me and Lilly come out alright. Let us become stronger because of it." *I am stronger, right? Right?!* I had to believe I was.

BENCH TALK

I called my mom after classes one Spring day. James and I had gotten back together but were on rocky ground. We had talked the night before and he asked me "What do *you* want?" A seemingly simple question. But I have this problem of thinking about what other people want or what I think I should want. It was probably just all a way for me to tip-toe around actually figuring out my issues and concerns. I knew I wanted to be with him, but I didn't know if I could be. *Is fear of getting hurt holding me back?*

I was on the way to take bus from campus to an open house with my future housemates and I needed to vent to someone. I shared most my concerns with her, about my struggles with religion, stress over homework and of course boy troubles. My mom told me that she and Lilly had had this exact conversation a few days before regarding a guy my sister was seeing. Her hypothesis made sense: we are afraid of getting close to someone because we lost the most important man in our lives and don't want to have anything like that replicated. I had wondered before whether my dad's death had a play in my relationships in general. I'm terrified of losing people, getting out of touch or ever having to say goodbye. Maybe, by dating James, I feared he might replace my dad. *Would letting another man into my life like this make my dad a background figure? Would my connection with him slowly dwindle away?* I already felt like all the little strings that connected me to him were fraying. I had stopped surfing as much which was something that always made me feel close to him. I had started questioning religion in a way I never thought I would and I suppose I had always associated Christianity with my dad. I wondered if by losing one, I would lose the other as well.

When we got back to the dorms after scoping out a house downtown, I texted James. I tried to sound casual about it, saying "Hey, I've figured a lot out. Wanna talk?" when really I had to calm myself down after a small emotional breakdown. Nervously, I waited for him to come down the stairs of his dorm building and we walked out onto the beautiful sunny knoll. My heart pounded, hands shook and tears began forming, threatening to roll down my cheeks at an alarming rate. We sat down on a bench in silence. I knew if I opened my mouth, my voice would shake and I would have to make myself vulnerable. So that's what I did. I sat there taking breaks between sentences to keep my voice steady and he slid across the bench to wrap his arm around me.

ABSTINENCE

In the summer, we held hands and kissed and I slept at his house almost every weekend, even though we still weren't having sex. I always told myself to wait until marriage because I wanted to save one thing for the person I was going to spend the rest of my life with. I had said that so often and it now just sounded like a rehearsed phrase, one that had little meaning. At times I questioned whether refraining from sex was even logical. But I saw it as the one last bit of abstinence I had yet to break so I stubbornly held onto it.

I had already drank and smoked weed, but only after I spent a significant amount of time thinking about why I abstained from them in the first place. During freshman year I opened myself up to a whole other world that I never really experienced in high school. I saw drinking and smoking in a different view and no longer based my decisions around whether or not God, or my Christian peers back home, would approve. I had started figuring out what I wanted. I still had a great time being sober but I found they just added new perspective. *And besides,* I'd tell myself, *my dad was a total stoner.* I remember finding his bong in the backyard and having no clue what it was until a few years later.

SUNRISE

So there I was sometime during winter quarter of my sophomore year laying in bed with my first love James Sutter on just another Saturday morning. Outside the birds sang and the sun rose, but inside my heart beat fast and tears rolled from my eyes. I was what one might call an "emotional wreck." I had been battling myself for so long, telling myself to be strong, not to give up or let go. I feared what might happen if I did. *If I finally realized in my heart I was no longer a Christian, would that moment just cut the final string keeping my dad and me connected? Since Christianity got me through so much, did I owe something to it?*

James wrapped his arm around me and said nothing. He looked at me with that respectful, concerned expression that gave his face a slightly blank look. This was the face he made when he knew not to say anything and to just be there. I looked at myself from the outside. I saw the wall I had never quite destroyed guarded by my stubbornness. I saw a little girl praying to God every night to keep her strong. I saw my jumbled thoughts like a mess of colorful yarn all tangled up. I saw my dad's smiling face. And I knew I had to let go.

I let go of my fear of loss. I didn't know whether or not God existed. I didn't know if all along Christianity had just been a crutch for me. Maybe because I believed God would help me, I was able to help myself. Maybe that faith I put in Him, was actually faith in my own strength. I didn't know that the questioning never stopped. I didn't know a lot of things.

But I did know I would always be my father's daughter.

UNDER THE EUCALYPTUS TREES

Our blue tent sits in the grass on the edge of the trail this time, instead of the old orange one with the open screens that seemed to glow at night like a jack-o-lantern where we were the candles. The wooden picnic tables have more carvings and accidental burn marks than before and by the base of a eucalyptus sits a large brown metal box to keep the foxes away from our food. Those crescent leaves still flutter in spirals from peeling white branches and when you step on them they still crunch.

The first time we came to Santa Cruz Island was ten years ago, accompanied by our adventurous dad. He took us for a week over Thanksgiving to camp beneath the eucalyptus', swim in the glistening bay and catch lizards with little lassos made from tall grasses. The island had advanced since then with more amenities, visitors and animals. We'd changed with it, gaining with time more knowledge and experiences.

I sit on the edge of the worn-out table by our

tent, in jean shorts, a flowery tank-top and no shoes. I toss my dusty feet back and forth, feeling the air rush past the blisters on the back of my heels. Lilly grabs food from the shiny metal bin and I carefully step into sandals to help her. After a day of peanut butter and jelly sandwiches we begin preparing our favorite camping meal, one that we had eaten all through our childhood in the desert, the snow and the mountains. I fill our water bottles and rinse off two forks in the spigot a few steps away.

Earlier today, Lilly and I had decided to do an eight mile hike to another bay. All our previous trips to the island took place when we were too young to trek along the cliffs and we were excited to explore further. I filled up my CamelBak, laced up some new hiking boots and strapped mine and Lilly's bathing suits to the little bungees on my pack. We lathered on sunscreen, zipped up the tent and headed out on the path towards the small bay where the trail started. I couldn't help but remember walking along that path for the first time. It had felt like stepping into a new world; white butterflies fluttered in loops and fuzzy black and yellow caterpillars and scuttling blue-bellied lizards bathed on the sunlit dirt trail. That was the first time I had seen eucalyptus trees and the first time I had heard the call of a meadowlark. Strolling along it now so many years later seemed in itself a dream, a surreal blending of the past with the present.

We finally arrived at the bay, the clear sky meeting the deep blue of the Pacific Ocean in the distance. The beach from this view looked rocky, but the closer you got to the water the sandier and softer it got. An empty dock stretched into the water and on both sides of the bay were towering cliffs. The one to the right was where the trail to our hike began, a series of switch backs until you reach the summit. When we made it to the top, sweaty and hot with no shade for relief, I could feel blisters forming on my heels. Normally my stubbornness would have gotten in the way of saying anything, but blisters are those kinds of things that don't really go away and only become more unbearable and hellish as time goes by. When I mentioned it to her, with my head down and a red face from heat and embarrassment she stopped for a moment, gave me her camera and ran down the mountain. I saw her little spec down below, blonde ponytail waving back and forth until she finally become lost in the trees. The sun beat down and I looked over the vastness of the Pacific Ocean, trying to make out the California coast in the distance. We had never made it this high because we were kids who liked to draw and read on the beach and snorkel in the ocean with little sting rays and Garibaldi.

Revisiting old places is like watching memories being played out in front of you. The wind felt the same against my skin and made me close my eyes and smile softly at all the images of goofy kids climbing trees. I opened them and from the edge of the cliff where I stood alone I could see perfectly the dock where so many years ago we had unpacked all our supplies from the unstable little boat. Our dad had brought a red dolly and large plastic containers that held all our supplies for the week. The island had no running water at the time, so our dad put Lilly and I in charge of carrying the forty gallons of water to the campsite. The ranger helped him stack the containers and told us that there were only three other people on the island this week and in case of emergency there was radio in the empty ranch house.

From my view on the cliff I couldn't see that ranch house, but it's right along the path, crisp beige paint, white picket fence and red flowers growing under the windows. From what I remember it hadn't changed much. But beside it sat a new building, a small museum made for tourists about the history of the island. The abandoned shacks hidden in grass still decayed there, as well as little caves Lilly and I would crawl into only to find them full of bats. Down below I could see the rusting abandoned tractors and old farm tools.

We lazied around the camp site that Thanksgiving day until our dad came back from some wanderings with a huge walking stick like our own Gandalf and proposed that we write the three other campers invitations to a feast that night and deliver them. We took it as a project: let's draw turkeys on it, let's make it colorful. Let's do this and that until we finally got up and embarked on a tour of the upper loop campground. No one was home at their sites; we called and when no one answered, we left our notes under rocks on the tables, praying they would find it.

That night, beneath the singing eucalyptus leaves, our dad opened the ice chest filled with dry ice and took out turkey meat, much to our amazement, and other ingredients that escape me now. I do remember he brought a can of mandarin oranges which I could eat for days. We set the table with our mismatched utensils, candles and the gas burning stove.

Then two women made their way slowly into the camp, a mother and a daughter, all smiles telling us how sweet the invitation was. A little later a man came walking from the direction of the ocean and came over to the table. He had just returned from a hike and hadn't been back to his site to see the invitation but looked very pleased to be welcomed to a lovely feast. He ran back to his site to change and when he returned, we all began our own celebration and experienced a night that none of us expected to have. We were strangers who quickly bonded over food and memories. I can't remember the exact words said, though I do remember eating my orange slices out of a blue bowl and moths hitting the lights. They left that night, still thanking us for reaching out.

The next day my dad told us that the man who came was there by himself in memory of his son who had died a year before. He had decided that every holiday he would visit someplace that his son would have enjoyed. When he returned to his site to change and saw our invitation on his beaten up, lonely table, next to his one person tent, he was amazed that people who didn't know him, know what he looked like or his name, could know exactly what he needed. He would have spent the night alone with only memories of his late son to keep him company but instead he spent it with a father and his daughters, a mother and her daughter, and he felt the love of family.

Standing on that cliff above the Pacific and looking back on that sacred memory, I feel incredibly grateful for that night. I stood there lost in the view and in memories until I saw the little moving figure of Lilly as she began climbing up the mountain. She no longer ran, clearly exhausted and finally came panting up to me with an unnecessary amount of bandaids in her hands. We looked out at the ocean together as she caught her breath and gulped down some water.

Maybe this does not seem so special. When I told her I had blisters I had expected an are-you-serious kind of look on her face and a roll of the eyes. But none of that came from her. She ran down the mountain because she wanted us to make this hike together. I sat down on the trail and took off my socks to put on the bandaids. They had already swelled so bad that after another mile I ended up going barefoot the rest of the way, feeling guilty then that she did all that. But she never complained and once we got to the beach she helped me get across the rocks and we were victorious at last. We stacked pebbles and reminisced on those days when the island had no running water or flushing toilets. The past played before us, days of bliss when I think back to our childhood and that trip. I see the kids we were with our sticks and bandanas, and to who we are now and I can't help but smile and be thankful for the life I have. So many things about the island had changed and I realized that even though we were such different people now, we were still those kids who just wanted to poke purple and orange sea cucumbers and catch scuttling crabs by the shore.

So here we sit after a day of hiking and blisters, eating the combination of ground beef, mac 'n' cheese and baked beans. The sun inches closer and closer to the horizon, hiding behind the mountains as the air begins to cool off. We share the campground with countless other tents and hear distant laughter, but unlike that Thanksgiving night, we keep to ourselves.

At the end of that adventure ten years ago, the dock hand said to our dad, "You are a rich man." He considered it for a moment, thinking about how little this trip actually cost and then realized the man was not talking about money. Lilly and I clean up our little site, pack away the food and crawl into the tent. As I snuggle down in my sleeping bag next to my sister after an exhausting day in the sun and say goodnight to her, I think about what that man said and realize just how rich I am.

ACKNOWLEDGEMENTS

Thank you mom. If any relationship demonstrates how much people can change, it's ours. When I told you about this project, you said to write whatever I needed to. Together for too long we may fight, like driving through the remote highways in New Zealand, but you are there for me always. I see you as the epitome of a strong, independent woman. You took on the role of a single parent, and owned it.

I'd also like to give a shout out to my adventurous sister sis Lilly for sharing you wisdom and understanding my jokes. To James Sutter, for encouraging me to step outside of my comfort zone and to my best friend Jenayl Peters, whose trust and compassion always lightens my load.

UCSC Creative Writing Department, I love you. Micah Perks, your memoir class motivated me and helped me share my experiences through writing. You are honest and full of advice and I'm so glad you suggested I continue with this. Melissa Sander-Self, your positive attitude is such an inspiration and I feel privileged to have taken your classes. Thank you Emma Schmitz for being my writing partner in crime. And to Dan O'Leary and Mike Greer for your humor and honesty in small group workshops.

Michael Jara you are like a brother to me and have always been there to see me on to the next great adventure. Lori Peters, it was in 5th grade that I got something published in the paper and you began the spark. Both of you were there before the cancer, during and after and have always supported Lilly and I.

To my crazy family, the ones I am blood related to and the ones I am not. All my friends, the ones I grew up with in elementary school to those in high school and college, you guys are amazing. Words can not adequately describe how lucky I am to have the friends and the life I have.

Made in the USA
Las Vegas, NV
23 March 2021